THE LOADS OF POETRY PART 3

AARCHI ADVANI SAINI

Contents

Contents

Contents

Contents

Contents

Author

Aarchi Advani Saini.!

[ ] Author of the book "The Loads Of Poetry"

[ ] Social media "Aarchi Advani Saini"

[ ] Aries, believe in destiny.

[ ] Author of the book "The Loads Of Poetry Part One and Two", "The Journey of Love", "The Way to Love", "The Anonymous", "Let's be Confidante", "New Self", "Error", "The Cabalistic Child ", "Confession", "Dark Dead", "Half Dead", "Faith is All", "Anjaan Ajnabi", "Lifeless Life","Stuck", and more.

Author?

Aarchi was born in India in 25th March 2002, the daughter of Sanjeev Advani Saini and his wife Mamta Saini.

She becomes one of the youngest author of her hometown Shamli. For this Danik Jagran newspaper covers this news, Later, many news channels interviewed her. So renowned for "The loads of poetry). She has sold the book worldwide, the recipient of numerous prestigious awards in her writing journey. She writes daily columns syndicated throughout the world. Aarchi Advani is well known for her writing on many other platforms. She is also a fantasy and literary fiction author specializing in "Life", as well as her upcoming book "Dream".

She publish her 10th book as her Hindi novel called "papa".

She also hosts a channel where she uses her passion for storytelling. And a background in business to help other creatives navigate their writing. So she is compiling an anthology named, "Of Your Choice", And her publishing journey is another level, she is good at her writing skills, but no one knows how to write books, same with her, but with the passage of time, she grows. When she's not writing or tubing she enjoys listening to books,

Making stories on her own. And love to live in her virtual world.

1. "Life is not just about..."

Life is not just about...

Life is just not about sorrows and grief,

Its something u cannot explain in brief.

Life is just not about getting depressed and sad,

Its something to enjoy every moment like mad.

Life is just not about feeling lonely,

Its something like helping someone feel homely.

Life is just not about argues and fight,

Its something to enjoy life every day and night.

Life is just not about saying "why only me"?

Its something to change every I to WE.

Life is just not about being perfect,

Its something to learn and accept all facts.

Life is just not about wearing crown of wealth,

Its something to have a good health.

Life is just not about waiting for death,

Its something to live thinking every moment as ur last breath.

Life is just not about questioning Gods plan,

Its something to be an inspiration for all men.

Life is just not about being a master in every Art,

Its something to rule every Heart.

2. "Alone I Sit And..."

Alone I sit and keep on Writing

Thinking About my Mind And My Heart who are Fighting.

Alone I sit and see every where

And search for one with whom I can have my Feelings Shared.

Alone I sit and think of Life And Death

And feel the Pain that comes to some one when it is their Last Breath

Alone I sit and Dream And Dream

And feel as if I am the King And Queen.

Alone I sit and Plan to Work Hard

But it comes to a stop when I Don't Know from Where to End and from where to Start

Alone I sit and Talk With The Sky

And Aim to reach High

Alone I sit and Listen to Nature's Song

And feel that i have to go Very Very Long

Alone I sit and I Think very Deep

And in the midst of darkness i Silently Weep

Alone I sit and Wander about the Festivals And Fame

And feel that all that is in simply Vain

Alone I sit and hope that Success comes to your Feet

And send you all d good wishes that come at u to Meet.

3. "I want to.."

I Want to walk with the sky
And with the birds,I Want to fly.
I Want to sit alone and write
And want to be out of everyone's sight.
I Want to talk with the plants and trees
And listen to the sweet song of the Breeze.
I Want to forget all about the past
And want to move on very fast.
I Want to be free from all the servile bands
And Leave the footprints on the sand.
I Want to overcome the fear of fall
And want t0 have nothing, yet all.
I Want to rebuild the trust that was lost
And bring everything to normal at any cost.
I Want to make you happy all the time
And want to stop the poem,as i do not get any more rhymes.

4. "What a magician is he...!"

What a Magician is He...

What a magician is he

who created the Day and Night.

And made the world so beautiful

with all the colours so bright.

What a magician is he

who created the lands and trees

And made the watery oceans

lakes and seas.

What a magician is he

who created the Earth and the Sky

And made the men

with his ambitions so high.

What a magician is he

who created the leaves and grass

And gifted us the useful alloys

like Bronze and Brass.

What a magician is he

who created the Sun And Moon

And made the beautiful

Morning,Evening and Noon.

What a magician is he

Who created the Earth and Sky
And made the mountains
Majestically so high.
What a magician is he
who created the sweet recreation
And made the way to attain peace
Nothing else than Meditation.
What a magician is he
who created the cycle of Live And Die
And made Death a painful Truth and
Life a Beautiful Lie.
What a magician is he
Who created Great People, but very Few
And one of them whom i know
Is no-one else but YOU..

5. "Family"

Family
What is a family?
Well, something that's
Impossible to define
For words do have
Limitations, but feelings don't.
Family, a place where
Life begins and love never ends.
Where you can probably
Always find a helping hand.
How beautiful is the love
Of every member out there.
Where everyone teaches you
To love to care and to share
Little fun little masti little crazy.
All these ties us in a bond.
A bond of love
That lasts forever long.
How Lucky am i
To be a part of this wonderful relation
All i want is to thank Almighty,
For his marvelous creation... ☺

6. "A Friend like you.."

A friend like you
A friend like you
Is undoubtedly a beautiful gift
And what else i desire
Just a long lasting friendship.
A friendship that knows
No boundaries no limits
And what else i desire
To be with me every minute.
A friendship that sustains
All ups and downs.
And what else i desire
Just be the jewel in my crown.
A friendship that has seen
All smiles and tears.
And what else i desire
To help me overcome my fears.
A friendship that is
Praised and admired.
And what else i desire
To have a friendship that's never expired.

7. "Down the memory lane"

Down the memory lane
Today, my mind takes me back
To those mornings -8'O clock.
Where we were all ready
With our uniform-the blue frock
With those neatly combed oily hair
And with those ties, shoes n sock
The mind planned with the schedule
Just to roll and rock.
And desperate to see our friends
To walk and talk.
Oh those school days
Were so very nice
And those lunch breaks
With chips, burgers and fries
Or sometimes even homemade
Food like vegetables and rice
And apart from all the fun,
Even studies going smooth and wise
Everyone their, with ambitions
So high to touch the skies
All those memories are

Decently stored in the cart
And trust me, these memories
Will never go apart
For all these are there
So deep in the heart
And i just wished to refresh them,
By song, write up or any kind of art
But at last, i wish that
Life had a button to 'Re-Start'

8. "The empty chair"

the empty chair

How strange is the cycle of life and death

You probably dont know which is your last breadth

But still, death has its own threat

Although death lies in a body, not in relation

But how strange is this God's creation

Still you can do nothing else then being patient

Oh God ! This is just not fair,

One has got is enough pain to bare

For it is really difficult to see the empty chair.

Memories of them are present in every thing.

Be it any place or with any human being

And thus, we wish going to them by flying with a wing

Leaving the person you love is actually sad

And that feeling is really very bad

But all we have is tears to shed.

Oh God, this is just not fair

One has got is enough pain to bare

For it is really difficult to see the empty chair

But to communicate with them, now we lack

Coz they are on a completely different track

Although we wish we could bring them back...

9. "World of dream!"

World of Dreams

Oh boy, lemme take you to the world of dreams

Where you are my king and i'm your queen

Where we are free to fly, run or swim.

A place where there's magic in the air.

Where we have got is no pain to bare.

Everything there is simply bright and fair.

But does a place like this exists

Oh yea, oh yea

It does...

A place where we can see our wishes come true

And Bring back the times that just flew

And enjoy watching the flowers grew.

But does a place like this exist,

Oh yea oh yea

It does...

A place where I'll be yours and you'll be mine.

And together we'll dance and sing in the sun shine

And everything will be just perfect and fine.

But does a place like this exist

Oh yea oh yea

It does...

10. "Out of the box"

Out of the Box
Honestly, when I did open
The link stated there
Just didn't thought it would be
So exciting to stare.
Looking at it made me realize
That even nothing means all
All that is upon you that
How you fill the empty hall
Your thoughts are the key
For any of your worry
But all you need to do
Is be patient, not in a hurry.
Now it is upon you
To design the canvas that's plain
And make it so powerful
That it's ignite be as a flame...

11. "Kindergarten school Times"

Kindergarten School times

Today when i look back

and remember those wonderful times.

When we started learning alphabets

numbers and rhymes.

A strange feeling

always running in the mind.

But fortunately the people out there

were very patient and kind.

But as the time passed

We became familiar out there.

And slowly and steadily

we learnt to care and to share.

And now i feel not to extend this much

just say it in a short summary.

That those wonderful moments with them

are merely an unforgetttable memory.

12. "Back to the past"

Back to the past
How speedily the time flew
Didn't realize how fast we grew
I just didn't knew.
But still, some words left unsaid
Some voices were unheard
Some things were unseen
I wish we could go back there
Where we would have ample of time to spare
And everything there would be simply fair.
The time spent with the one's so dear
Where 'We'll apart' was the only fear
But today, even physically far, we are near.
But still, some words left unsaid
Some voices were unheard
Some things were unseen
All those lovely moments, stored in the cart
And that is why, even if miles apart
Our friendship is bonded by heart
So don't you ever Say goodbye
Bcoz, goodbye's are meant for another Hi !
For our friendship knows no limits, just like the sky

13. "Hold my hand"

Hold my Hand
Hold my hand and i ll take you there
And together we'll make a wonderful pair
Let us go somewhere out
Where we can fly with the clouds
Or can even swim or sing aloud
A place that's got something beautiful to see
Where there would be no-one else, only you and me
And together we'll sit in the shade of the tree
Just hold my hand and i ll take you there
And together we'll play with those teddy bear
A place where life won't be restricted to a room
Where we'll see the flowers gloom
And we'll dance on the musical tune
We'll walk leaving the footprints on sand
And will be just free from all servile band
Where we'll be the master of the sky and land
Just hold my hand and I'll take you there
And together we'll make a wonderful pair
A place where everything is yours my friend
Where we both shall walk hand in hand
And hope that this journey never ends.

14. "A New You"

A New You
For me,
Perfection is U+I=We
Perfection for me is,
Being happy with your own deeds
And removing all those unnecessary weeds.
And stop making those big Tension's heaps.
Perfection for me is,
To be real, no more fake
To give yourself , a much awaited break
And be someone's icing on their cake
Perfection for me is,
To be someone's helping hand
and act differently then those usual trends
and also be free from all those servile bands
Perfection for me is,
distancing yourself from all the drama
And experience every Trauma
but never let your story end, always put a Comma.
Perfection for me is,
Nothing but Being true
Although you are smart enough, i Knew
So simply, Perfection is creating a new YOU !

15. "Stolen innocence"

Stolen Innocence

Oh ! You standing out there

Yes You !

Let me tell you something's that's bitter but true

and lemme explain you why am i not the same as the rest of the few.

None of you know me by my name

And you people consider me as your country's shame

But i am merely an animal thats tame.

Even i want to live a life as happy as yours

My deeds may be wrong, but trust me heart is divine and pure.

Will you please help me getting all these cured ?

I am also no fool

But instead of books, we are surrendered by those tools

Even i wish to go to those lovely schools

But whatsover, this is our fate

And we are supposed to do it, even if we hate

because this will bring us a food or plate

Anyways, thanks for listening to me

And for sparing some time thats free

And i hope together we'll make a change

not You, Not I But WE !!!

16. "What do I write.?"

Why do i Write
Many a times
It comes to my mind
When i sit outside
In the light of sunshine.
That, why did I
Start to write
And why do i always prefer
To be out of everyone's sight
And why do i like to be
Introvert and quite.
Why am i more comfortable
To write than to talk
Or simply thinking while
Taking a long walk
Or simply relaxing
While sitting on the rock.
But then i finally
Found the answer
That every person other person
Is a master
Is either a poet,
Singer or dancer

To be friend with your
Own self is also an art
Coz you are never alone
Your companion is your heart
The one who can never
Leave you apart
So once in a day, spend some
Time sitting in the dark
Or go out somewhere
Like rollerblading in the park
Or simply observe the
Flying birds and dogs that bark.
So always remember to
Be 'ONLY YOU'
Don't change yourself
For one or two.
For people who remain
True to themselves are very few...

17. "A happy ending"

A Happy Ending
Love someone who knows
all your flaws and fault
But yet thinks that you
are his choice- The default.
Love someone who can be
with you till the end
Who, at times become your
caretaker, guide and friend.
Love someone who holds your
hand for a while but heart for life
At the end, you need to
proudly say, I am his wife.
After all, love is not about
only celebrating valentine's day;
Its when your love increases each
day seeing those hair's grey.
A happy Ending doesn't need a
happy beginning.
After all, behind every loss
is hidden a deeper feel of winning

18. "All I wish to tell you"

all I wish to tell you
Hold my hand when I fall
Listen to me when I call
Be with me in those crowded hall
Boost me up when I fail
Help me out when I wanna sail
Look at me when I go pale
Stand with me when no one's there
Have some time for me also, to spare
Also listen to me and let my feelings be shared.
Listen to me when I want to speak
Handle me when I sometimes freak
Also suggest me some new and interesting trick
Wipe my tears when I cry
Help me spread my wings and fly
And never break my trust, don't u ever lie
All this is no fake, absolute true
For I trust not all, but very few
And one of them is undoubtedly you....

19. "Goodbye"

Goodbye !
Never thought i'd bade you a bye,
Just if Life could spare us one another try.
The journey of life is so unpredictable and confusing
It is like tossing a coin, either winning or losing
I cannot imagine a moment without you, my dear
As we have shared the deepest of the smiles and tears.
No matter where our life leads me
I'll be in your thoughts, in the deepest of the sea
My Memories will always linger in your mind
And I shall meet you, whenever or wherever you find.
No matter what happens, I will hold your hand
For I am with you till the very end.

20. "My last words"

My Last words
I want to die with my
Memories and not dreams
I want to be the jelly on
Someones ice cream.
I wish to tell them
I did care a lot
But to show them
It was never taught.
I wish to tell them
Even i Do love you
And hope all this
you already knew.
I wish to tell them
Not to cry coming to my grave.
For i am always with them,
Either in the wind or wave.
I wish to tell them
My last words
That I wanted to be
one of those Free Bird...

21. "Tell, what you feel?"

Tell , What you feel
Communication is actually
An integral part of life...
It should be in the most clear way
With your daughter, mother or wife.
Express what you feel
rather than bashing.
Hiding away doesn't make you
more cool or dashing.
Show how much you care
Before it gets too late
Because you are just a prisoner
In front of your bad fate
Our heart stores feelings
That are way in depth
But we never know
when is our last breadth.

22. "The world outside the pane"

The World Outside the Pane
Once in a while,
Go near to your window pane,
And watch out the people
walking through those multiple lanes.
Talk to those Chirping birds
And listen to the music of breeze
Don't limit your thoughts
and let them be squeezed
There's a whole new world
If you can see
Let your imagination grow
And let it swim in the deepest of the sea

23. "Angels"

Angels
Spread your wings and fly,
For you are an angel in the paradise.
You are meant to reach there, so high
Go and touch the horizon, the splice....
Spread the colors of Joy to each place
For the world needs more of your smiles
The people have been running in a never-ending race.
They don't know what they left while running miles and
miles.
Ask the almighty for a little mercy, a little support
For he is the only savior of ours
The Judge of our court
And we are his slaves, imprisoned in his bars.

24. "My Dream Boy"

My Dream Boy
Every day and night, he is
Lingering in my mind.
But he is just a dream,
In reality, i still didn't find.
Coming with a bouquet
Full of roses and daisy.
But his image in my mind
is not clear, a little hazy.
He sits on his knee and
proposes me for being his wife.
And asks me to take that special
place in his life.
Butterflies in my stomach
make me go crazy and insane
It was as if the wild wind of love was
pulling the stormy rain.
That feeling is just too beautiful
to describe in any line
Every heart beat of mine had just one thing
to say, "Just to make him mine"
When i opened my eyes,
my dream disappeared

I couldn't judge, was it something
strange or weird ?
But one fine day,
I'll Find my dream boy
For he is the one who will fill my Life,
With all the colours of joy

25. "Memories of her"

Memories of her
Why is that my fate
Always betrays me
Why it gives me a barn land,
when I asked for a Flowery tree.
Why does it always leaves me
in the maze of sadness and pain.
Why it gives me a stone
when i asked for some edible grain.
Why it does
sheer injustice to me, always
Why is it that she leaves me in a while,
while it's just her memories that stays
Why is it that I cannot
flush her off from my mind.
And why is that LOVE is always,
Deaf dumb and blind..

26. "Never break their heart"

Never break their heart
Never break someone's heart
Never cause them pain
For once they leave,
You'll never see them again.
Just think for a while,
How much they loved you
And their love was also no joke,
Like yours, It was just so true...
They get scattered into pieces
When you left them alone
Every bitter word of yours,
Hit their heart like a stone.
Dont get too much attracted to
All the material things
For once in life, they'll
leave you and will cut your wings.
But people like them remain with you
at every stage, in every way.
For they are the one's that will hold you
Till our hairs turn grey.

27. "Lucky are those"

Lucky are those...
Lucky are those who have
parents to take their care
For, its- indeed very difficult
to see their empty chair.
How difficult it is to
even imagine such a life
And it's like someone has
ruined your life with a sharp knife.
Lucky are those who have their
parents hand on their head
For the orphans are merely
a living body that are mentally dead.
Just think for a while
and you shall feel a huge breakdown
Now understand, how these people hide
their real pain inside a mask, like a clown.
You won't see your parents now,
or will either here their voice
But we are helpless in front of him,
After-all we are merely his toys
Every moment of their life, is
like a curse

And every second the situations

turns out to be worse

28. "If I could go there"

If I could go there
Only if Life had a button to
rewind and go to the past
I would stop the time that's
running so fast.
Going back to the days
I remember the most
Where the entire days passed by
Sitting calmly at the sea coast.
The time that give me
bundles of joy
Where our only desires were
having new barbies and toys.
Only if Life had a button to
rewind and go to the past
I would stop the time that's
running so fast.
Today, we are longing
to go back there
Where everything was so
Unbiased and fair.
But the time that's gone
can never come back.

And it leaves behind,
none of its track

29. "From dreams to reality"

From dreams to reality
Every other day, my dreams
were getting fade and light.
It went away somewhere
far away from my sight.
Some factors proved a
great hindrance for me.
It's like they shook the
roots of my tree.
Now, I thought i'd have got is nothing
to do but sit and cry.
But instead, I chose to
give my life, a new fresh try.
Every thing happens for a
reason, nothing goes in vain
You can never know the hidden
happiness, even in the deepest of the pain.
So, think of something
and you shall find some talent in you
For, the people who rise after a
great fall, are very few.

30. "Have you ever"

Have you ever
Have you ever watched
the beautiful sun set
It is one of the most
spectacular view I bet.
Have you ever smelled
the aroma of the first rain
It has a hidden magic in it,
which makes you forget all your pain.
Have you ever heard the
sweet song of the birds
Their voice is so adorable,
even though they don't utter a word
Have you ever tasted the
most spectacular food cooked by mummy
Every bite, your taste bud shall pass on a
single message, "Its tooo Yummy"
Have you ever touched
the waves of the river.
It is so cold and freezy,
It can even make you go shiver

31. "Don't you ever"

Don't you ever
Don't you ever cry
coming to my grave
For I am with you forever,
In the wind, in the wave...
Don't you ever mourn
when i die
For I'll be watching you
From those blue skies.
Don't you ever feel
distressed and alone
For i'll be with you always, but
in a way that's completely unknown.
Don't you treasure and preserve
me when i'm already dead
For, our bond is strongly
tied with a strong knot of thread.
Just cherish me when i
am standing by your side
For its no use watering the plants,
once they have died.

32. "Message in a bottle"

Message in a bottle
On one fine day,
Walking along the sea side
The place where I have
laughed and even cried.
I saw the tides pulling a
bottle along with the waves of the sea
And i thought of taking the bottle,
and opened it, sitting on my knee.
There in, i came across a
a message from someone to his dear.
But it seemed he could not handle her
this message, he might be in a fear.
I started reading it
and could literally feel his emotions
He had so much love for her,
somewhere more deeper than these oceans
Anyhow, i wanted those two
patient hearts to unite
As the beautiful sunset of the day,
merges with the shining night.
So i started to find
any possible clue

And inside it, i found an
address, written with a ink of color blue
I stood up with a
hope in the heart
For, I knew very well,
how difficult it is for true lovers, to stay apart
I was in a state of shock
when i read the address of his dear
I was in the most beautiful phase of life,
where i could laugh and even roll down my tear
The whole message in the bottle
belonged to no-one else but me
And at the end it read,
"Can't it be like - U+Me = WE"
And then, i saw him
standing there nearby
Waiting for my answer
looking at me with a cute shy.
I could not afford
to lose him in any way
For i knew, our love shall grow deeper
even when our hairs turns grey...

33. "Come back"

Come Back
If only u could come back to earth,
For now, we understood your presence was worth.
You gave us your extra care and love,
so now it's difficult to see your grave, white as the dove.
Although you'll always be in our heart,
but, physically now you are far apart.
Why did you leave us alone,
Without you, we feel so distressed and alone,
Just come back for a while, or take us with you
Because, we feel alone every time, even with a crew.

34. "Mother Nature"

• 41 •

Mother Nature
The darkness is fading
and spreading the light
And the atmosphere nearby
is so serene and quiet
The warmth of the sun light
is touching my face
And i can hear the birds
going for a prey to chase
The weather
is so pleasing and nice
And nature lets us feel it,
without paying any price
I can smell the coolness
of those green grass
And now i feel,
this time should never pass

35. "I love you"

I Love You
Who says love is only
for girlfriend / boyfriend.
When I say "I Love You"
Do not put your thinking to an end.
Love is in the air,
Love is sharing, understanding
and care.
Love is life,
Be it with your parents,
friends or wife.
It is too beautiful
to explain in words.
Love's everywhere,
In humans, animals and birds.
So, my dear friend
Saying I Love You
Doesn't mean only
A thing or two
For i am blessed to have
some great people as my friend
And i hope that
our friendship never comes to an end.

When your love touched my heart,
I felt like friends like you never apart
Bcoz my feelings for you never fade,
Just want to tell you something- only a few
That all this I wrote is no fake- all true
And at the end, i wanna conclude
That my dear friend, "I LOVE YOU"

36. "Dreams"

Dreams
Dreams, are like a chaser
And you, need to be a racer.
They can knock you in any form
And can leave you even, leaving behind a storm.
But every time, they leave some opportunities to grab
All you need to do is, hold it tightly, like a crab.
You are never too old to build a new dream.
But, don't you stick to a particular stream
Open your doors and they shall knock you soon
And can convert each of your curse to a boon.

37. "Change"

• 45 •

Change !
I know the quote sounds strange,
Yet, in life, the most constant thing is change.
Believe that everything that change is for a reason
And every sorrow or happiness we face is just for a bad season.
For change means first, be better than what you were before
change means changing the direction of waves, not shores.
For i think change is necessary, after a short time
And i feel to get to an end, as cannot get any further rhyme

38. "Left me"

Left me !
When I needed you the most,
You were busy at your own post.
When I was lost in the dark
You were busy with your own spark !
When I needed you at my side
You were happy with your material pride.
When I wanted you to handle my swings in mood
Instead, you just goofed and behaved very rude
When I wanted a tight hug and a sigh of hope
You denied and just even didn't cope
When I asked you for a new try,
You left me heartbroken, just with sadness and cry.

39. "Walking away!"

• 47 •

Walking away !

Walking away from you, leaving some old memories behind.

For, there was nothing left to cherish more, at least I didn't find !

Walking away from all those trauma and pain,

For, I found nothing but every try in mere vain.

Walking away from you was difficult but i had to chose

It was because there were ample of difference of views.

Walking away because relationships cant be forced to be tied

For in the most difficult times, i didn't find you at my side.

40. "Express and explain"

Express & Explain
Express your imagery
on the canvas of art.
Explain your feelings,
from the core of your heart.
Feel the beauty of nature
and the life of your surroundings
Don't let your imagination
be impressed within your boundaries
Express your thoughts to people
in every possible way.
Explain what you want to represent,
and let your words only say.

41. "Lost eyesight"

Lost eyesight !
People says,
The sun rise is the most
spectacular view you can see
Leaving behind all your
sorrows and griefs, and just
sitting near the beach of the sea
But, God didn't wanted me to
be fortunate enough for
looking at the nature's beauty
Although, he is smart enough to
provide me a special sense
fulfilling his duty
But honestly saying my friend,
I never complained about the stuff
that i never got
Instead I thank the almighty
for all those special
things he brought.
Only if life spares me
a single day to see
the beautiful Earth.
May be not this time,

but i'd surely insist him to return
me my eyesight in the next birth.

• 50 •

42. "Take me there"

Take me there
Take me there,
Where love is in the air
Where we are addressed as one of the most adorable pair
Where people envy me by your love and care
Take me there,
Where happiness touches our feet
Where the birds comes just to greet
Where we can paint our destiny on a blank sheet
Take me there,
Where i can distance myself from all the pain
Where i can even dance with you, in the rain
Where we have nothing to lose, nothing to gain

43. "Just why?"

Just Why ?

My life's mess without you

And all this, you already knew

Then, why did you left me in this dark

I feel like, lost inside an ocean, surrounded by shark

Why didn't you understand what I wanted to tell,

I thought at least you'd understand me well.

Why did you prove me wrong, and betrayed me ?

Have you forgotten all those promises we took, under the shade of tree ?

How can you move on so easily, leaving everything behind

Have you seriously flushed me out of your heart and your mind ?

Didn't you even ever feel to come and clear your doubts

Or, you have just thrown me out of your heart, your house ?

Then, don't you expect me to come when you'll be calm

For the pains you gave me can't be healed by any of your balm !

44. "A place"

A place...
A place so beautiful and divine,
A place that has its own majestic shine.
A place so beautiful and mesmerizing
A place that's strongly recommended and advising.
A place that one longs to go
A place where you soul shall glow
A place that's truly stated as the summer capital
A place that is the home for some beautiful animal.

45. "Friends, a boon or curse ?"

Friends, a boon or curse ?

Choose a friend wisely, but then don't ever question his plan !

For, friendship is a bond that is for an eternal span

Being selfish and rude will break our beautiful fabric

Because, this will build some walls, of concrete brick

For a friend is a gift that is really adored

For they really create a musical chord

But don't you lie, just preserve our relation !

And never let it weaken, just build a strong foundation.

46. "As a Child"

As a Child

As a child,

Thousands of memories to treasure

Where the weigh of happiness can't be measured

Where most of the times were spent in mere leisure

As a child,

I remember my own good times

Where we were engaged in silly sweet crimes

Where life was not at all confine

As a child,

I remember those innocent smiles

Where we would enjoy in our own lifestyles

Where we were the reason for the people to compile

As a child,

I remember being center of attraction for all

Where we build the bridges and not the walls

Where every royalty seemed so tiny and small.

47. "Social vs real"

Social vs Real

The world has resorted to social media

Where you can find almost anyone, like an encyclopedia

But, at the same time, it distanced you from the people around

You find the one's lost, but lose the one's you already found

Friends for name, thousands in your list

But real friends ? Probably you can count upon them on your fist !

48. "Easy vs Difficult"

Easy vs Difficult

Easy is to judge someone's deeds

Difficult is to pull out your own weeds !

Easy is to say anything without thinking for a while

Difficult is to understand the pain inside a smile

Easy is to hurt someone who loved you truly

Difficult is to understand your mistake duly

Easy is to cut someone's wings

Difficult is to share even smallest of the things

Easy is to apply an ointment on a wound

Difficult is to rise again after falling on the ground

Easy is to break your precious relations

Difficult is to again build a strong foundation

Easy is to get angry and argue and burst

Difficult is to bend down and apologize first

49. "A story unheard"

A story unheard
We laughed
We cried
But you were my hero,
My mentor my guide !
We argue,
We fight
But I thought of you
every day and night
We concluded,
We got separated
But I was in a hope,
I simply waited
We moved on
We began a new life,
But yet,
You continued to strife
You realized
You asked for forgiveness
But this time, I gave up
Didn't wanted to be your witness
We brought up a story,
But didn't have a perfect end

Because all this was too
complicated to be mend.

50. "oh stars.!"

[Oh stars,]

Oh stars,

Don't you shine tonight

Don't you shine so bright

Leave me, just be out of my sight

Oh Stars,

Everything is now in vain

Because I am surrounded by the sadness's rain

But please, Don't you ever expose my pain

Oh stars,

Even I shall fall asleep, very soon

You go and be with your moon

And dance with him, on your musical tune

Oh Stars,

I have nothing left now, just to weep

For she's in my heart, in the corner that's deep

And its obviously difficult to make a sudden huge leap.

51. "Lingering scars"

Lingering scars
Years later, wounds may have healed
But my lips are still silent and sealed
My eyes looking for justice, for a new hope sigh
And my soul still looking for them, up in the sky.
My heart filled with tears to shed
For now I am just a body that's mentally dead
All the things changed, so rapid and fast
But still, my mind engaged in the past
Still didn't believe you are with us no more
And every passing day, I miss you from my heart's core.

52. "An Angel without wing"

An Angel without wing
When everything in life was a mess,
And when I was completely frustrated and stress,
You stepped in with a new sigh of hope
And you were ready to hold me and cope
I didn't expect such kindness from you, to be honest enough
Even then, you were with me, it wasn't something easy, very tough
You gave me ample of memories to cherish, and forget the pain
You taught me, after every storm of sadness, comes the happiness's rain
Now, I am convinced you are an angel to me sent from above
For almighty can't be with all, so he send you with his blessings and love.

53. "A Family"

A family !
Some words were still unsaid,
Some words were still unheard
Some feelings were still not expressed
A family that was idle for me has now became a war zone
Happiness, that used to reside here is now completely thrown
A family that gave me memories to cherish throughout the life
And now, they ended up having disputes between mother, sister and wife.
A family where I'd probably always find a helping hand
And now my dream house is like those muddy castles in sand
A family where we lived and laughed and enjoyed
And now, I feel there are some damages, many void
A family that used to be my home, my pride
And now, it's the reason a part of my heart has now died
Will they reunite?
Will they patch up among themselves once more
Oh God ! Please give me back
My precious gems that I adore.

54. "Friends for life"

Friend for Life

Friends are either,

For a reason or

For a season or

For lifetime !

Alone I can cry,

With others, I can try,

But with you- I spread my wings and fly

Alone I can swing

With others, I can sing

But with you - I feel like a King

Alone I can say,

With others, I can pray

But with you - I can forever stay

Alone I can't make a huge leap

With others,- I can reduce my pain's heap

But with you - I can laugh and weep

Alone I can be strong and brave,

With others - I move like a wave

But with you - I can stay forever until we reach our grave

Just be with me till the end

Have some spare time for me, to spend

And just an appeal - Forever, be my Friend.

55. "I Wish"

I wish
People say, Wishes come
true when you drop a coin
So I'd also ask for something,
Do you even wish to join ?
Let's ask for a life filled
With all the colors of joy
Repeat after me,
Oh you silly boy !
Let's ask for a life
that contains my paradise
And I am ready to pay
any amount of price
Let's ask for a life
Where I am my own creator
If anything goes out of track,
at least I won't weep later
Let's ask for a life
That i wished for every day
And i'd thank you
in every possible way
Don't give me the royalties,
I don't wish to be a king

rather, I wanna fly high,
Just give me wing.

56. "Introvercy"

Introvercy

May be I can't initiate a conversation with all

May be I can be put into introvert, they call

May be I cannot assure you or can show you that I too care

But, people think I am heartless and thus leave me with pain to bare

May be I cannot put on my ideas in to sentences that can be pleasing

But that does not mean I do not have emotions or feelings

May be I don't have the talent to be friendly in just a fraction of time

But that's Ok ! Don't let me feel I have committed a crime

I can't change myself completely, at least you should help me try,

If you can't wipe my tears than please don't be the reason to my cry

57. "Raise a Toast, Cheers !"

Raise a Toast, Cheers !
Hurray,
It's a day when you stepped in here
And people related you in the category of Shakespeare
A poet, that came up with some of his great read
Where emotions, sometimes happy or sometimes tears to shed
Come on all, let's celebrate your glorious occasion,
Bring on the wine and party at your nearby location !
Let's raise a toast to you for your celebration
And we hope you write till our last of the duration !

58. "Chocolaty, Chocolaty !"

Chocolaty Chocolaty !

People say I am very lazy,

But when I see cakes, I go crazy

My taste buds takes me on a completely new way,

And every bite just says, I Love You Bae

A completely chocolaty cake with icing, yum !

Deliciously baked with added love of my mum

Every bite has a chocolaty tangy taste

And I hardly can afford it to waste

Chocolaty chips decorated with artificial decorations and gems

I believe in sharing, but when this is concerned I forget even my friends

Just taste it once, and I am sure you'll fall over it again and again

For it will first touch your heart and then fit in your brain !

59. "Travelling"

Travelling
Life's not just restricted to a room
Widen your thoughts, enlarge them, zoom !
Travel as many times as you can, as far as you can go
For, there are places that will let your minds blow
Travel, with your own self, parents, sibling or spouse
But don't restrict your fantasy in just your house
There's a lot of adventures waiting for you to see
Just have a visit once, and you shall also agree
Engage yourself in all the adventures almost all
Or go to see the mountains, the caves or water falls
In short, be like the bird that knows no limit
What are you waiting then, Go and grab your ticket !

60. "An Angel"

An Angel
A couple of years back,
You stepped in this world, my cutie pie,
An angel sent from above, with his emotional cry!
Fluffy and chubby, I wish I could eat you my sweety
And trust me, You were more cute than Bugs bunny and
Tweety
Watching you grow up everytime was a blessing
And handling your drama's while eating and dressing
When you started to crawl, and talk- Sheer music to my ears
The time we rejoiced and celebrated and I shouted Cheers
When you first said "Pearl', my heart seemed to skip a beat
And that moment when you stood up on your feet
The times with you, when I become a child
And enjoy with you, being silly crazy and wild
Having a younger brother like you, was the most beautiful gift
And those endless joys while walking, when you hold my
wrist.
Your smile is the cure for any of my pain and trouble
Your presence vanishes my weariness and makes my joy
double
Didn't realize how fast the time flew, and now you are turning
7 soon

But everyday, we thank the Almighty for this sweet little boon
!

61. "Depression"

Depression !

People now-a-days have come up with a new idea, a new term,

And now have turned their minds weakened, that once use to be firm !

Depression, A disease they call, has just occupied a void in their mind

And it has made a huge impact on their senses, making them deaf and blind.

Being alone is a joy, but surrounding by negative vies is not appreciable act,

May be you may feel this rude, but my Friend, this is a natural fact !

Why complicate things when they are already so simple and nice,

Why do people think of you absurd when you are kind and wise

Life is too simple, don't make it complex and compound

Do not apply ointments on places where you have got no wound

Forgive and forget, not for their sake, but for a selfish motive only

Be surrounded with the people even, rather than being sad and lonely !

62. "Death leaving us apart"

Death leaving us apart
A day when I will be no more
When my place in your heart will be a pore
And you'll miss me with every passing day
And for another chance, you'll beg and pray
But, the time that's gone shall nevernever return back
The path once lost will never leave its track
So just cherish me when I am alive standing at your side
Just tell me your feelings, don't let your words hide.

63. "Companion for lifetime"

Companion for lifetime
No matter if the world laughs at me,
I'll hold you forever
No matter if the world thinks I'm childish,
I'll hug you tightly.
No matter if the world thinks I'm absurd
I'll love you forever
For,
It was you who smiled every time looking at me,
It was you with whom I could be so happy and feel free
It was you with whom I enjoyed having snacks with tea
For,
It was you who remained when almost no-one was there
It was you who tolerated my dramas, chose me to bare
It was you with whom I had always made a wonderful pair
You are my teddy, My friend
Because you stood with me till the end
And with whom, I had most wonderful time to spend

64. "Don't try to..."

Don't try to bury me,
I'll be back again with a new ME
I'll sow my own seeds and will
reproduce like the tree
Don't try to discourage me,
For i am like the spring
I'm ready to face the ups and downs,
Like these children on the swing.
Don't try to condole me,
for i have lost is nothing yet
And I'll reborn from my own ashes,
Just you wait and watch, I bet

65. "Parsis, a Minority !"

"Like sugar sweetened milk
We shall mix with you people there"
Said a group of people with a
Different dress, unusual hair
Keeping their words, they settled
With others and thus made a huge leap
Not many in Number, but obviously
A major group, with a great heap.
Zoroastrians they call themselves
Followers of Zarathustra the great !
A community generally recognized as
Quite unusual, weird - not straight
Finding happiness in everything
Exaggerating the matter in all the way
Just a glass of wine and freshly cooked
Meat, enough to make their day.
Scattered in different parts of nation
Yet having the roots same
Enjoying being lethargic,
Playing carrom- their fav game
Unusual names, generally spelled wrong
Like godrej and Tata
Believing to always choose a Brand, be

It Titan, Raga, or sonata
Words different and thus forming a
New version of a language known
And their voices sweet enough or
Sometimes even a mannish tone
Preserving their own culture, bringing a
New taste in it, adapting the new tradition
To eat, drink and enjoy this gift of God
Our life is their only mission and vision.

66. "The lost me"

The Lost Me
Everyone around me discussing,
about grades and marks.
And thinking about increasing
their fame, their sparks.
Deep inside, I am busy
finding the ME that I once lost.
And thinking to mend the broken
stuff, just at any cost.
Am I insane ?
Am I a fool ?
No, it's just that I love
my pen, instead of a tool !
People around me, thinking to
opt the most reputed place.
And, I am busy thinking to go
for a road untaken, leaving behind my trace.
Folks besides me are planning
for a life is comfort zone.
Simply to be away from paying
back for the housing loan.
Am I silly ?
Am I dumb ?

Even i have a life,
a heart- don't treat me as a numb !

67. "Headache"

headache
Ohhh this pain
Unbearable and intense
Makes me irritating and tense
Feels sometimes
Just to remove that shitty part only
The most safest option, that time is to be lonely
Ohh this headache
Sometimes I feel, it'll be the reason for my death
For it is not gonna leave me till the last breath
Ohhh this migraine
For the sake of Almighty, please go away
Whatever my mistake be, I had enough to pay
Ohhh this pain
I beg for Mercy, leave me for now please
This pain is now making me stiff and freeze.

68. "[A year before today,]"

A year before today,
Life gifted me the most wonderful blessing
A sweet little baby
To fill our life with all the colours of surprise
And pleasing everyone with your emotional cry
Sweety pie
You are my world, my love
An angel sent from above
Come let's rejoice and celebrate
The most precious moment of the year
Your momma and dadda will plan the best
For you to celebrate and cheer
But no gift can equal to the one
You gave us, my baby
You gave us a reason to live
You gave us the most renowned relation
You make us complete
Remember just a thing
We love you more than anyone here
All we wish is, may your life be filled
With all the joys, not a single tear.

69. "I'm a fighter"

I am a fighter
I will fight
Till death takes me with it
I will fight
Till I will be fine and fit
Why should I be
Quiet when I'm right
Why should I sit in the darkness
When I belong to that luminous light
I urge you people even
Stand up and shout
Don't you worry about the
People, don't get any doubt
Fight for yourself
No one's gonna stand for you
The best people are the one's that
Stand apart from the crew.

70. "Mentally Handicapped"

Sad times, everyone ready to blame him

May it be simply a physical pain in the limb

Always questioning him, Oh God, Why only ME?

And crying before him, sitting on your knee

Have you ever thanked him, for a small curve on the face

Remembered him even once, at anywhere at any place

Humans tend to blame than to appreciate

Finding the bad is an art for us

Discouraging someone, making them

mentally handicapped, you discuss

Change your way of seeing,

You'll have to pay for your deeds

Because the plant shall grow one day

by the sowing of your seeds

Don't push anyone beyond their limits

neither let them feel sad

For he's noting your work,

Don't add them in the list of bad

71. "The lost love"

The Lost Love
Better to live alone,
Than to live with people like you
Is this what you call a family ?
It's where the love stayed
a place where I was raised
Just those good old days
You people scattered my life into a part
You people just tore me, broke my heart
Just why did you do this ?
Why did you spoil my Life
Why always indulged in strife !
Can't you people stay happily,
adjust a little
Why let the fabric of
the family be brittle
Oh God !
Death's better then this
They have snatched my bliss
Oh God !
Give me ample of pain, I don't care
Fit me inside a room, restrict my life to a square
Any pain would be beautiful if I see that lost glare

I beg for Mercy, I will pay for their sin
Paralyze me from my feet to chin
But please, a new family hope- Begin.

72. "[Not necessary]"

Not necessary
That we Like each other all day
But yea, at least respect each other
In every possible way !
Respect is just a way of adding
Some more goodness in your nature
After all we are humans
The most wise creature
But yea, before respecting others
First learn to respect you only !
Be with the people who don't let
You feel lonely
Respect is earned and not
Taken with granted, as you generally take
So act wisely and peacefully
Taking a long awaited break

73. "My Savior"

My Savior

I don't know weather people believe in you or what they think

But I understand, you can change everything just in a blink.

Every time I rest my case to you and you bring out the best way

And you are the one whom I admire, I believe, I pray

Jesus, you've helped me always, expecting nothing in return

And you've made me realized, that even the worst situations can turn

Your presence is felt in every small thing, every place

And leaving behind some of your positive trace

Everything is easy when you are at my side

And there's nothing before you for me to hide

Just an appeal, be with me always as you have been

And with you, every loss seems a victory, everything I win...

74. "Scattered Heart"

I wish you could see
the depth of the love in my eyes
And could also see the pain
inside my smile, the tears, the cries
I wish you could feel
my feelings, before assuming anything
And could understand the reasons,
behind my mood swings
If you come and tell me,
I was just an option for you
And now when you have found
someone else in your life, someone new
You really scatter me in pieces and then
ask me to calm and be practical & wise
And your basic priority is to aim high
get success and reach the skies
Didn't think that you could be so
selfish and rude to me
And why do you think that I'll bind
you, never let you free.
Never do this to someone, never
break someone's heart, it hurts, a lot
If you truly love someone, hold them tight

don't weaken the strength of your knot.

75. "[God is also a great magician,]"

God is also a great magician,
creating such beauty like heaven on earth
And visiting there, paying any amount
to have a glimpse of it would be worth
Having a house near to this, away
from all the drama and toil
And we can proudly admit,
I belong to this place, this soil
Seems like fairy tales were describing
this place only, so serene and nice
And i wouldn't mind visiting it
once twice or even thrice.

76. "Phoenix in me"

• 92 •

Phoenix in me !

My wounds have now become my strength

And know I'll bloom from them at any cost, in any length

I'll reproduce from my own ashes

From the wounds, the patches

You left me thinking I'll be broken and scattered

But now I am not at all flattered

You will wait and see how the tables turn at you

And I'm not bashing, I shall prove this all true

Just wait and see how you'll face your own deeds

And the grasslands you grow shall be your weeds.

77. "Books, Books, Books!"

Books, Books, Books !
Books, Books, Books !
Of different sizes, contents and looks
The key to happiness,
read and feel
they are my survivor.
my heal, my meal
Books, Books, Books !
The key to happiness lies within them
They are the most precious gems
They neither complain nor demand anything
but they may turn you to a prince or king !
Books, Books, Books !
Be it fiction or fantasy, I have always loved you
Because, whatever the situation be, you are loyal and true.

78. "Am I grown Up ?"

What ?

You mean to say I am grown now ?

I mean, till now I was a kid, then How ?

You mean I'll be engrossed in a monotonous Life ?

And indulge in all those strife ?

No play, No time to spare.

No no no ! This is just not fare

All day filled with the work and duty...

No time to look at the nature's beauty

Studies till my head starts to ache

And live among these wicked people so fake

Aah !

Childhood was a blessing

Just playing, enjoying and dressing

Please, give me back those times, i ain't grown up yet

Just a few more years, I lend a debt

I can't afford to lose the most wonderful age

For I can't spend the entire life in the frustrated cage

79. "Unsung stories"

"I love you from my core
And this feeling, wanna feel it more
Your absence makes me feel like having a pore"
Message like his in his textbox roared
But, Alas !
This was just a draft
Hitting his heart like a shaft
The message that contained his thought
In her cage, he was caught
But his feelings to her heart, were never brought
And thus came an end to a wonderful tale
In the ocean of feelings, he could not sail
Because, in expressing his thoughts, he did fail !

80. "Truth of life"

Truths of Life

Lost in the dark, finding the lost ME

Shivering with failure, from heat to knee.

Losing my confidence, that once used to be my pride

My eyes, now searching for someone, who can be at my side

Tired of living among this wicked group of people

Who can't provide you a helping hand, instead make you feel cripple

Why did the time change ?

Why did it make me strange ?

Will you help me overcome my fear ?

I will co-operate in every way, I swear !

People who promised to stay, left away at the most crucial times

I was someone even less than ordinary, for me, they were supreme & prime

The most unexpected people stood, whom I expected the least

And now, I found out-Real friends ! Probably I could count them on my fist.

81. "Is death dangerous?"

[Is death dangerous ?]

Is death dangerous ?

Is death having a threat ? .

Have you ever faced death and came back ?

It'll be like your Life will run on a completely new track !

Touching that threat and even then living is not a small thing
!

For, you need a lot of courage, and that's not possible with all
the being

Just enjoy every of your moment you live

Have ample of blessings and love to give !

82. "A friend to count upon !"

Friends come and go

But the one's who shall stay

can probably never ever know !

One such friend, whom I could expect

the least, entered and became a gem of my life

Times with him, I always feel relaxed and happy,

forgetting all my pain and all the strife

Helping me with all the weird problems,

Always available to talk

A big Hi5 to you,

Yo Bud ! You rock

Talking about almost every single

issue that we face in day to day

I don't know about all, but certainly

I am relieved, a friend like you will always stay

Having a sweet and cute personality,

You are one of the most trustworthy person I met

And our friendship shall grow deeper

and wider every passing day, I bet !

Roshan, Roshu, Roshanahmed

like your name you are antique and unique

But I can certainly never know how the time

passes by, all the days and the week

83. "An Orphan's Complaint"

Once upon a time,
Passing by the sea side
I saw a kid crying,
eyes full with tears, blue and wide
Asking the waves to just
go away at once, away from him
And just muttering one thing,
Why didn't I learn how to swim,
Going near to him,
I asked him what was disturbing him so much
But he was in his own world, without
giving a response about my voice or my touch
Then, I asked him again,
"What is the matter with you, dear ?"
But he could not open to me instantly
Was looking at me in a fear.
I assured him I would
be doing no harm
And then asked him to
get a little calm
He said in a very sad voice,
"I'll never ever forgive this sea"

Even if it's waves begs for
forgiveness, touches my knee
Why did the tsunami snatched my parents,
Thus making me an orphan and alone
Hearing this, I could not control the tears,
neither his nor my own
Why is this injustice to this poor kid,
Oh God ! There's plenty of other evil and bad
Many people committing crimes are running
free but this poor kid, away from mum & dad

84. "Broken Dreams"

Broken Dreams
My life stuck up in circuits and digits
Limited my imagination to only formula and physics
Lost the capacity to think, out of the box.
And my creativity has vanished, mind hard as rocks.
Just walking along a way where destination is nothing new,
Merely like a slave of my destiny, that once I myself drew.
Please don't make this mistake, don't lose your talent and dream
Don't be under someone's feet, It's your life, stand up and scream
For once your dreams are lost, you'll never see them again
And then, each of your efforts- you'll count them as just a vain.

85. "Chit chat"

[Chit Chat]
Chit Chat
May be is not our cup of tea
From this band, we are always free
Introverts ! It is a blessing given to
only some people, including U and Me
We are surrounded in our own thoughts,
lost in the feelings of sea !
Writing becomes our friend,
where we can express what we feel
They are our actions, our
happiness, and our heal
May be people around us has
changed the view of looking at us
They don't appreciate the
trial of ours, our guts !
How difficult is it sometimes
to even get surrounded by a few
And this is what we cannot change in a
second, with this feeling only, we have grew

86. "The memories"

The Memories
May be she wasn't destined to be in my life
But memories of her shall always remain
They'll give me a moment of happiness
when I'll be surrounded in the ocean of pain
Her memories means her mere presence to me
They are the answers to my questions, my key
Oh God ! Your actions are never questioned, always trusted !
Although sometimes it makes you feel cripple and busted
Yet, I believe you have gave me something that'll remain forever
But please, let the memories be with me, do snatch them never

87. "The hardest part of friendship"

[The hardest part of friendship]
The hardest part of friendship
When we bade each other that "GOODBYE"
But, I knew you are now all set to
pursue your dreams and touch the sky
All those wonderful times,
now just a memory to cherish
And think how fast and speedily
did the good old times perish
Everything going so smooth
but yet, sometimes feeling like a pore
Every way is open but sometimes
seems like some closed doors
The good times flew
Did they leave a trace ?
Or is it that we are just running
in a never ending race
Sit for a while and
think going to a flash back
Look for the pores,
the holes the crack
Don't you look at the circumstances and wait

Heal them before its too late

88. "Destined to meet but not to stay together"

May be destiny had some different and incomplete plans for us

And so you were never destined to be a part of my life, thus !

We met may be to get separated, meant for teaching me the true colors

Not every time, magic prevails, sometimes there are just no wonders

But, was I just an option to you ?

That in a fraction, your love flew !

And now You found some other

And your conscience just didn't bother ?

But know when we have finally chosen different path

And left me just in a state of awestruck and wrath

Just remember for once, the times we spend- those beautiful days

And those love quotes, you dedicated and I praised

Those sunny days, when we sat under the shade of the tree

And now, all this just remained in my heart as a memory

You were the beginning and middle and the end of my book

But may be now the copyright of it, someone else has took !

89. "The lost charm of friendship"

The Lost Charm of Friendship

I wish we could change the words once spoken

I wish we could mend the hearts once broken

But, why do we always indulge in an endless strife ?

And why do we consider this blessing as just a game, Our LIFE !

At once, inseparable friends and now stranger !

It's just our Ego's that are throwing us in this danger

Can't we find a middle way out of it, just be friends again

We are we ourselves being the cause of our pain !

Think about those good old days, when we lived for each other

At times when we fought like siblings but also cared like father & mother

Just why are we bringing our ego's in our relationships. these days

And then losing the charm of friendship in this weird maze

90. "Existence in your memories"

Existence in your memories
One day
I'll only exist in your memory
A memory that
will linger in your mind.
And for my death
you shall hymn
You will have no
track of where will I be
And from them,
you shall neither hear me nor see
Some day, I will be just
a bird, that's free
Time will eventually fly
and you shall thus get what I was.
And then, you shall get to know
how much you have loss.
But, you will just have to regret
somewhere- it was you who may be the cause
So, just tell the ones you love
make them feel special and dear,
For they're gone, the only

thing that'll be left with you is tear
Thus, tell me at once, when I am
with you, at you side, somewhere near. !

91. "Dealing with our imperfections"

Dealing with our imperfections
When we unite,
It's a merging of our souls
When we are on our way to
achieve those desired relationship goals
But we knew perfectly,
neither of the two are 100% perfect
And this fact has neither put a band
and we never bothered for it or affect
Dealing with each others imperfections
that's the essence in our relationship build
And with each passing day, we shall pour
more of love in our jar and make it filled

92. "A place where there was snow on the air"

[A place where there was snow in the air]
A place where there was snow in the air
Where the people had time for me to spare
A place where there were rivers of chocolates and sweet
Where the colorful birds were flying above me just to greet
A place where there was the aroma of magic
And always away from the toil, trouble, the tragic
A place where I could live as I wish
Where life wasn't restricted to a dish
A place whose existence is still a question mark
Where there was the hidden aroma of glamour and spark

93. "Lizzy"

Lizzy
Look at the wall !
You'll find her crawling there
But don't you do any harm to her
I won't spare you, I swear
She's my companion, My lizzy
the one who's with me till he end
May be you'll find it weird
But yea, she's my friend
Always with me, follows me wherever
I go, at any pint of time
And I am certainly sure she'll
follow me to the jail, I committed a crime
U may think it absurd but animals are
too one of the best friends if you can make
For humans can leave you once
but animals can never let your heart break
Small in size, yet the best of all
is my friend lizzzy, my sweety
And I would love to make more such
friends, be it tom or jerry or tweety !

94. "Adore you always"

Adore you always
I'd keep you with me
no matter how much
life transformed
You were a beautiful
part of my life
But may be we were never
meant to be together
At least you'd always
be with me, close to my heart
Sharing you with no-one
just make you mine
Hope you could turn yourself
into a gemstone
and I'd always always adore you, my dear
Be mine and stay
with me forever
if only you could
be a gem stone

95. "[The day when you stepped into my life]"

[The day when you stepped into my life]
The day when you stepped into my life
everything's special since then
But that magical evening with you
hits my memory again and again
The day you and I were together
away from the hustle bustle and the toil
Spending time with each other, no one
around us to disturb or to let the good times spoil
When we went to the church, the mall
did shopping, had a meal together after long
The day you were in so good mood, you
performed a dance, and dedicated a song
The day you asked me to hold that
special place in your life
To fill the void in your heart and
asked me to be your wife
I wanted to shout and let the world
know that I love you
But there was no one to listen to us,
It was just we two
The next moment, you asked

for my hand, and gifted me a ring
I felt like the top of the world
wanted to fly spreading my wing
Yo mean everything to me now
my love for you increases each passing day
And I know we'll be there to hold our hand,
Even when we grow old, when our hairs go grey

96. "Till the end"

Till the end
Our love is not like the castle in the sand
no storm or thunder can break the bond
This is what I always use to say, when we
sat on the outskirts of the town, near the pond
Little did I knew that for you, love is just a game
And it can be played with anyone you wish to
Is this what love means to you? Seriously
i was unaware about this, I had just no clue
Did all my feelings mean nothing to you?
Are you a person having no heart?
Now i get the point ! Everyone is merely an animal
And in ruling them, you are a master of the art
But remember one thing, you shall have to
face your own deeds !You'll Reap what you will sow
Sooner or later, this shall flung you back
anytime in the near future, probably not now

97. "Did I Expect a lot ?"

Surrounded in a small world of my own
I was satisfied in my paradised zone !
Then why did my life changed, why you came to my life,
Like an angel, doubling my joy and ending my strife.
Least did I know and believed that this is just a temporary
hope
And all stories doesn't have a happy ending, like in the daily
soap
But, then! was it that i expected a lot from you ?
And in a moment, your affection faded and flew
I thought that yo were there for me when no-one else was
And you accepted me the way I am, ignoring my flaws
Alas, I was just an ordinary for you, but you meant a lot to me
My best friend my wellwisher, my guide, a lot you see
Better late than never, I realized I was better alone
For, now your feelings didn't heal my pain but they groan

98. "Satisfaction"

Stop putting yourself into other's place and
you shall unlock the doors to all your pain
You'll never be satisfied if you go on searching
for the snowfall when it's thunder and rain
Be happy with what you've got
never feel disappointed and sad
Something's are not meant for you
but for all the stuff you have, be glad
Look around the world and you'll find a
lot of people suffering still spreading joy
Stop comparing your happiness and trauma
with others, just stop being annoy
See the world with a new hope, a new sight
And you'll feel a change in yourself and every where
Just follow the righteous path and then suddenly
you shall feel God by your side, with a shining glare

99. "If I told you!"

If I told You !
I wish I dared to tell you
that I had a different plan
Not everyone aims to be
a doctor or engineer, man
Sometimes Life isn't the way
you wish it should be
Not every thirsty crow
always comes near a sea
But I expected probably you
could see the sorrows i hide
But sometimes I'd better bury my
dreams, when they affect your pride
Deep inside, it leaves me in a
state that I can never get rid of it
However hard I tried, somewhere
my heart had to admit and said "I Quit"
If only I had the guts to tell you
that i had a different aim, a different goal
I would be much happier, and not experiencing
that void in my heart, stinging me and creating a hole

100. "Biggest failure"

Biggest Failure
Failures are a key to a new try
And they lead yo to a level that's high !
But, sometimes, Life gives you a huge break down
And you have are left with nothing, but a drown!
Once a day, I experienced the same failure with me
And i was forced to fall flat on my knee.
Everything seemed to have misguided its way
And it was as if Life had chosen only me for its prey
Everybody started to think i was now a loser
And even my colleagues thought i was a tamed user
The business had a huge loss to pay, for my silly mistake
And then, my company busted on me, like a heavy earth quake.
I had no option left other than asking for a new chance,
But deep inside, i hoped if they would looked at my efforts, by a glance.
Rather than a new try, they left me in the dark,
Then, I found a hope of spark
I finally learned that, behind every loss is a sigh of a new hope,
I finally found some new opportunities, some new scope
Just learn from your failures and you will find some thing new

For, you will never realize when did your opportunities just came & flew !

"lost Myself In Finding You"

Lost Myself in finding you

Losing you was a matter of luck

you were not destined to stay with me

And I had to digest the fact that not

every story has a beautiful end, you see

Least did I know that i had already united

with you from the soul, my heart and mind

And now, it's so difficult for me to get that when

I lost you, it's like I lost my soul, now hard to find

Every of my heartbeat had your name etched in it

And now you see ! How can I live with a heart that belonged to

you

Every day without you, is like a journey that has no end,

Every now and then, my life annoys me and I feel blue

Why is this happening to me ?

Why did I lose myself, finding you !

Why is that your memories remained

While the time just rapidly flew !